W9-DDP-390

STECK-VAUGHN

ACHIEVE

Indiana

English/Language Arts

5

TEACHER'S GUIDE

Harcourt Achieve

Rigby • Steck-Vaughn

www.HarcourtAchieve.com
1.800.531.5015

ISBN 0-7398-9920-1

1 2 3 4 5 6 7 8 9 10 355 11 10 09 08 07 06 05 04

Achieve Indiana
Contents

Program Features

With ACHIEVE Indiana, you can . . .

- help your students succeed on the **Indiana Statewide Testing for Educational Progress-Plus** *(ISTEP+)* English/Language Arts test.
- meet the mandates of the **No Child Left Behind Act (NCLB)**.
- monitor your students' **Adequate Yearly Progress (AYP)** in reading proficiency.

 Begin with Modeled Instruction . . . That Matches the Indiana Standards!

- items correlated to **Indiana** English/Language Arts standards
- instructional tips for all items that teach how to arrive at the correct answer
- **Indiana** Standards cited on every page

 Have Student Take a Practice Test . . . That Simulates an *ISTEP+* Test!

- each item keyed to an **Indiana** Standard
- content and design of the *ISTEP+* English/Language Arts test

 Follow Up with Additional Support . . . That Emphasizes the Indiana Standards!

- detailed answer explanations for all items—a further opportunity for instruction
- standards identified for reteaching opportunities

STANDARDS FOR *Indiana English/Language Arts*

Standard 1

Students understand the basic features of words. They see letter patterns and know how to translate them into spoken language by using phonics (an understanding of the different letters that make different sounds), syllables, word parts *(un-, re-, -est, -ful)*, and context clues (the meaning of the text around a word). They apply this knowledge to achieve fluent (smooth and clear) oral and silent reading.

4.1.2 **Vocabulary and Concept Development.** Apply knowledge of synonyms (words with the same meaning), antonyms (words with opposite meanings), homographs (words that are spelled the same but have different meanings), and idioms (expressions that cannot be understood just by knowing the meanings of the words in the expression, such as *couch potato*) to determine the meaning of words and phrases.

4.1.3 **Vocabulary and Concept Development.** Use knowledge of root words *(nation, national, nationality)* to determine the meaning of unknown words within a passage.

4.1.4 **Vocabulary and Concept Development.** Use common roots *(meter = measure)* and word parts *(therm = heat)* derived from Greek and Latin to analyze the meaning of complex words *(thermometer)*.

4.1.5 **Vocabulary and Concept Development.** Use a thesaurus to find related words and ideas.

4.1.6 **Vocabulary and Concept Development.** Distinguish and interpret words with multiple meanings *(quarters)* by using context clues (the meaning of the text around a word).

Standard 2

Students read and understand grade-level-appropriate material. They use a variety of comprehension strategies, such as asking and responding to essential questions, making predictions, and comparing information from several sources to understand what is read.

4.2.1 **Structural Features of Informational and Technical Materials.** Use the organization of informational text to strengthen comprehension.

4.2.2 **Comprehension and Analysis of Grade-Level-Appropriate Text.** Use appropriate strategies when reading for different purposes.

4.2.3 **Comprehension and Analysis of Grade-Level-Appropriate Text.** Make and confirm predictions about text by using prior knowledge and ideas presented in the text itself, including illustrations, titles, topic sentences, important words, foreshadowing clues (clues that indicate what might happen next), and direct quotations.

4.2.6 **Comprehension and Analysis of Grade-Level-Appropriate Text.** Distinguish between cause and effect and between fact and opinion in informational text.

4.2.7 **Comprehension and Analysis of Grade-Level-Appropriate Text.** Follow multiple-step instructions in a basic technical manual.

Standard 3

Students read and respond to a wide variety of significant works of children's literature. They identify and discuss the characters, theme (the main idea of a story), plot (what happens in a story), and the setting (where a story takes place) of stories that they read.

4.3.2   **Narrative Analysis of Grade-Level-Appropriate Text.** Identify the main events of the plot, including their causes and the effects of each event on future actions, and the major theme from the story action.

4.3.3   **Narrative Analysis of Grade-Level-Appropriate Text.** Use knowledge of the situation, setting, and a character's traits, motivations, and feelings to determine the causes for that character's actions.

4.3.5   **Narrative Analysis of Grade-Level-Appropriate Text.** Define figurative language, such as similes, metaphors, hyperbole, or personification, and identify its use in literary works. (Simile: a comparison that uses *like* or *as;* Metaphor: an implied comparison; Hyperbole: an exaggeration for effect; Personification: a description that represents a thing as a person.)

Standard 4

Students write clear sentences and paragraphs that develop a central idea. Students progress through the stages of the writing process, including prewriting, drafting, revising, and editing multiple drafts.

4.4.2   **Organization and Focus.** Select a focus, an organizational structure, and a point of view based upon purpose, audience, length, and format requirements for a piece of writing.

4.4.4   **Organization and Focus.** Use common organizational structures for providing information in writing, such as chronological order, cause and effect, or similarity and difference, and posing and answering a question.

4.4.5   **Research and Technology.** Quote or paraphrase information sources, citing them appropriately.

4.4.10   **Evaluation and Revision.** Review, evaluate, and revise writing for meaning and clarity.

4.4.11   **Evaluation and Revision.** Proofread one's own writing, as well as that of others, using an editing checklist or set of rules, with specific examples of corrections of frequent errors.

4.4.12   **Evaluation and Revision.** Revise writing by combining and moving sentences and paragraphs to improve the focus and progression of ideas.

Standard 5

At Grade 4, students are introduced to writing informational reports and responses to literature. Students continue to write compositions that describe and explain familiar objects, events, and experiences. Student writing demonstrates a command of Standard English and the drafting, research, and organizational strategies outlined in Standard 4—Writing Process. Writing demonstrates an awareness of the audience (intended reader) and purpose for writing.

4.5.1   Write narratives (stories) that: include ideas, observations, or memories of an event or experience, provide a context to allow the reader to imagine the world of the event or experience, and use concrete sensory details.

4.5.4 Write summaries that contain the main ideas of the reading selection and the most significant details.

4.5.5 Use varied word choices to make writing interesting.

4.5.6 Write for different purposes (information, persuasion) and to a specific audience or person.

Standard 6 **Students write using Standard English conventions appropriate to this grade level.**

4.6.1 **Handwriting.** Write smoothly and legibly in cursive, forming letters and words that can be read by others.

4.6.2 **Sentence Structure.** Use simple sentences *(Dr. Vincent Stone is my dentist.)* and compound sentences *(His assistant cleans my teeth, and Dr. Stone checks for cavities.)* in writing.

4.6.3 **Sentence Structure.** Create interesting sentences by using words that describe, explain, or provide additional details and connections, such as adjectives, adverbs, appositives, participial phrases, prepositional phrases, and conjunctions.

4.6.4 **Grammar.** Identify and use in writing regular *(live/lived, shout/shouted)* and irregular verbs *(swim/swam, ride/rode, hit/hit)*, adverbs *(constantly, quickly)*, and prepositions *(through, beyond, between)*.

4.6.5 **Punctuation.** Use parentheses to explain something that is not considered of primary importance to the sentence, commas in direct quotations *(He said, "I'd be happy to go.")*, apostrophes to show possession *(Jim's shoes, the dog's food)*, and apostrophes in contractions *(can't, didn't, won't)*.

4.6.6 **Punctuation.** Use underlining, quotation marks, or italics to identify titles of documents. When writing by hand or by computer, use quotation marks to identify the titles of articles, short stories, poems, or chapters of books. When writing on a computer *italicize* the following, when writing by hand underline them: the titles of books, names of newspapers and magazines, works of art, and musical compositions.

4.6.7 **Captialization.** Capitalize names of magazines, newspapers, works of art, musical compositions, organizations, and the first word in quotations, when appropriate.

4.6.8 **Spelling.** Spell correctly roots (bases of words, such as <u>un</u>necessary, <u>coward</u>ly), inflections (words like <u>care</u>/<u>careful</u>/<u>caring</u>), words with more than one acceptable spelling (like *advisor*/*adviser*), suffixes and prefixes *(-ly, -ness, mis-, un-)*, and syllables (word parts each containing a vowel sound, such as *sur-prise* or *e-col-o-gy*).

HOW TO USE *the Student Book and Teacher's Guide*

Modeled Instruction for Indiana

Achieve Indiana begins with Modeled Instruction, a section that contains a variety of practice items similar to items found on the *ISTEP+* English/Language Arts test. In this section, students will practice answering multiple-choice items, short-response items, an extended-response item, and a writing activity. Following each item is a Tip that models for students an effective way to arrive at the correct answer. Also, for your easy reference, a correlation of each item to the Indiana English/Language Arts standard can be found at the bottom of the page.

You can use Modeled Instruction as independent practice and let students work individually through the items and strategies. You can also work through the section as a guided instruction activity in small groups or with the whole class. Discuss each item and how the accompanying Tip focuses the student on what the item is asking and how to arrive at the correct answer.

On pages 13–19 of this guide you will find **Answers and Explanations for Instruction** for each item in Modeled Instruction. The explanations afford an additional opportunity for instruction and are written in language you can use directly with your students. They give details about the correct and incorrect answer choices and can be utilized with individual students, as you guide small groups, or the whole class.

Practice Test for Indiana

Beginning on page 43, *Achieve Indiana* includes a Practice Test that follows the content and design of the *ISTEP+* English/Language Arts test. The Practice Test consists of 38 multiple-choice questions, 4 short-response questions, one extended-response question, and one writing activity. Each multiple-choice question is followed by four options, one of which is correct. Students will answer the multiple-choice items by filling in circles next to the correct answer. Students will answer the open-response items and writing activity directly in their student book.

Answers and Explanations for Instruction for all items in the Practice Test are found on pages 20–30 of this guide. Each item is first identified by the Indiana English/Language Arts standard that it tests. Then, explanations are given for the correct and incorrect answer choices. These explanations provide an additional opportunity for individualized instruction.

Rubrics for evaluating the open-response items, extended-response item, and writing activity are included at the end of Answers and Explanations for Instruction on pages 31–37.

ADAPTING ACHIEVE INDIANA INSTRUCTION
for Use with Students with Special Needs

Every student can benefit from reviewing test-taking strategies and taking the *ISTEP+* English/Language Arts practice test. Three types of students, however, require practice tailored to their needs.

Struggling Readers, by definition, are not reading on the grade level at which they will be tested. These students commonly read at least two grade levels below the testing level. When a struggling reader reads aloud, you will undoubtedly observe the student's lack of reading fluency, difficulty sounding out grade-level words, and failure to recognize common sight words. Struggling readers often read so slowly they cannot keep track of a paragraph's or even a sentence's content. This seriously hampers their ability to comprehend what they read. Because some of these readers have no diagnosed learning disabilities, they may not receive accommodations such as more time to test or assisting devices such as dictionaries.

English Language Learners (ELLs) present a unique challenge because their levels of reading proficiency vary greatly. Some are fluent readers in their native languages and transfer these skills readily to English, but still may be puzzled by idioms and figures of speech. Others, like struggling readers, read below grade level and are still trying to master word-level comprehension.

ELLs also face unique challenges in taking tests. First, ELLs may lack the background knowledge necessary for full understanding of a passage if it relies on unfamiliar cultural experiences. Second, vocabulary and concepts common to a specific grade level might not be in place in the second language. Third, literary grammatical structures may not resemble the oral language with which they are familiar. Finally, the testing format is often unfamiliar in the home culture.

Although it is impossible to remove all testing obstacles for these students, most test items are written to avoid idioms and ambiguous language. To the extent possible, test items are written to avoid reliance on prior cultural knowledge.

Students with Specific Learning Disabilities (SLDs) usually have average or above-average intelligence but are often hindered by some level of language difficulty. Students may have trouble with semantics, phonology, syntax, or morphology; these types of difficulties are often interrelated. Students with problems in one area will likely have problems in another area. Students may struggle with input, or receptive language. They may have trouble distinguishing letters, or they may read lines repeatedly or skip lines. Other students receive language smoothly but have trouble organizing it. These students struggle with sequencing and have trouble inferring meaning from texts. Other students have memory deficits in working, short-term, or long-term memory.

Some SLDs cause output problems in spatial orientation and fine motor control, meaning that students may test well but have trouble recording answers correctly in standardized test answer booklets. Many students with SLDs must also overcome a lack of motivation and confidence as a result of years of academic struggle. They frequently rely heavily on teachers for guidance and require a great deal of positive reinforcement.

Because these students have identified disabilities, accommodations can be made for them in testing and in practicing for tests. Students' Individualized Education Plans (IEPs) identify appropriate accommodations, including more time to test, alternate forms of recording answers, and the use of assisting devices such as dictionaries and calculators.

Test-Taking Strategies for Students with Special Needs

The test-taking strategies on pages 11–12 of this guide are appropriate for all students, and some are particularly useful for struggling readers, ELLs, and students with SLDs. For example, underlining key words helps distractible readers target important terms and drawing pictures of abstract concepts can help auditory learners and ELLs make sense of content. Model these procedures for students and provide them ample opportunities to practice using them. However, you may need to go beyond general strategies to help your students with special needs succeed. The following suggestions are appropriate for many students with special needs.

■ Use simple sentences that avoid slang, idioms, and negative phrases as you teach these strategies. Speak slowly and pause at logical points to give students time to process and discuss what they hear. Provide written instructions to reinforce verbal instructions and define any terms that may confuse students. When possible, use graphic organizers.

■ Help students build word webs or word banks that explore and link operational words common to test items. For example, a word web for *contrast* would include words and phrases such as *difference, distinguish, tell apart, unalike,* and *compare*. In math, a word web for *add* would include *altogether, sum, plus,* and *in all*. Tell students that learning these words in groups will help them decide quickly and accurately what a test question is asking. Encourage students to look for and underline these key words in test questions. This strategy is particularly helpful for ELLs.

■ Help students make a chart of common words and suffixes that identify test items such as *compare* and *contrast*. For example, *-er, more,* and *less* form a group that implies comparison and contrast, as do *-est, most,* and *least*. Students should recognize that test items might not use the actual words *compare* or *contrast*.

■ Give students applied practice of tested skills. For example, show students a picture of a common, easily recognized item such as a house or a dog. Ask students to describe the object. What color is it? How big is it? What details can they list? Then show students a picture of the same object that is a different style or type. Have students compare and contrast the two objects. Have students find as many similarities and differences as possible. You may want to use a Venn diagram to record these ideas.

As students become more proficient, guide them through similar exercises involving things they know well but must recall from memory: two musicians or two movies, for example.

■ Ask students whose test-taking skills have improved to guide other students through several test items. Putting the process into their own words by teaching a peer will reinforce the process and build their confidence. Supervise the students' explanations, encouraging them and augmenting their explanations when needed.

■ Teach students to access their prior knowledge about passages they read, math problems they work, and the testing process in general. Use practice test items to lead students to recognize that the items are like many others they have completed in class or on homework.

■ Since the test format itself may intimidate some students, help them achieve a sense of ownership by using the white space on the test pages to their advantage. Reduce students' anxiety by encouraging them to mark on test items, underlining familiar terms, drawing pictures or diagrams when these are helpful, and showing their work as they eliminate incorrect responses.

■ Help students develop strategies for pacing themselves during the test period. Students with special needs can get stuck on a test item and spend too much time on it. Teach students to use a watch or clock to monitor their time.

Time management includes knowing when to skip an item and move on, returning to the skipped item if time allows. Teach students how to skip items and return to them. Students with output processing SLDs especially worry about leaving answers blank and need explicit practice in matching answers to the correct lines.

■ Teach students to break long test passages into more manageable chunks. Practice with students reading a paragraph or a few sentences and underlining key words and phrases. Have students write notes in the margins of the passage to help them remember where key information can be found.

■ A similar strategy can be used for decoding long words with prefixes and suffixes or compound words.

■ Work with students to discover the meaning of unfamiliar words and idioms from the context of the surrounding sentences.

Additional Strategies for Students with Specific Learning Disabilities

■ Review each student's IEP to learn what accommodations are permitted during testing, or ask the student's counselor to provide a list of accommodations. Use these accommodations during the practice test so the student will not be surprised during the actual test.

■ Teach behaviors that help students return to the test item by interrupting their work on the test item, then returning to the beginning of the item rather than picking up where they left off.

■ To alleviate students' anxiety, ensure that the practice test environment is as close to the actual test environment as possible. If students are allowed to record their answers orally on tape, be sure they do so during the practice test. If they are allowed to use manipulatives or assisting devices, be sure to provide them during the practice test.

■ Teach students to segment complex instructions. For example, if a test item requires an extended response that asks students first to compare and then to draw conclusions, model how to find each instruction and mark it, perhaps as "Step 1" and "Step 2." Guide students as they respond to one step at a time and encourage them to review the question after they have recorded their answer to check that part of their answer matches each step. This strategy can also help struggling readers and ELLs.

■ Model each test-taking process and strategy explicitly and repeatedly. Students with SLDs need guidance, repetition, and positive feedback as they tackle standardized testing situations.

PREPARING STUDENTS FOR *the ISTEP+ Practice Test*

Before giving the Practice Test, take some time to discuss these test-taking tips with students.

General Test-Taking Strategies

Time Use
- Don't spend too much time on any one item

- Work rapidly but comfortably

- Return to unanswered items if time permits

- Use any time remaining to review answers

- Use a clock to keep track of time

Error Avoidance
- Pay careful attention to directions

- Determine clearly what is being asked

- Mark answers in the appropriate place

- Check all answers if time permits

Reasoning
- Read the entire item or passage and all choices before answering

- Apply what has been learned

Guessing
- Answer all items on the test

- Try to eliminate known incorrect answer choices before guessing

Test-Taking Strategies for Multiple-Choice Items

The *ISTEP+* English/Language Arts test contains 38 items in multiple-choice format. Specific strategies can help students work through the multiple-choice items most effectively and efficiently. Here are some helpful strategies to discuss with students.

1. Read all directions thoroughly before answering any items. Misinterpreting directions can lead to incorrect answers.

2. Look for and underline or highlight key words as you read through the passage and item.

3. If an item seems complicated, draw a diagram or picture to represent the item. This can make abstract or confusing concepts seem easier to understand and manage.

4. If an item seems too difficult to answer, skip it and move on to other items. Later, the question may seem easier to answer. If you skip an item, also skip the space for that item in your book. When you finish the test, go back and answer any items you skipped.

5. Make sure your marks are clear and dark and erase any mistakes as thoroughly as possible.

Test-Taking Strategies for Short-Response Items

The *ISTEP+* English/Language Arts test includes 4 short-response questions. These strategies can help students work through the short-response items effectively and efficiently. Discuss these strategies with students.

1. Write legibly and clearly.

2. Identify and mark key words as you read the passage and item.

3. If an item seems difficult, create a diagram or picture to represent the item. This can help make confusing ideas seem easier to understand.

Test-Taking Strategies for Extended-Response Item and Writing Activity

The *ISTEP+* English/Language Arts test includes one extended-response item and one writing activity. These strategies can help students work through the extended-response item and writing activity effectively and efficiently. Take some time to discuss them with students.

1. Write legibly and clearly.

2. Use available space to plan your responses before you begin writing. For example, you can create webs, outlines, or diagrams and take notes for listening.

Administering the ISTEP+ Practice Test

Be sure that each student has the following materials before testing begins:

■ The student book

■ Pencils (with erasers) for marking answers

The test is administered in four sessions. It will take approximately 3 hours and 10 minutes of class time.

Session	Preparation Time	Testing Time
Test 1	5 minutes	31 minutes
Test 2	5 minutes	29 minutes
Test 3	5 minutes	55 minutes
Test 4	5 minutes	55 minutes

Answers and Explanations for Instruction

MODELED INSTRUCTION

Test 1

Think Like a Horse (pages 4–8)

1. ● **Correct. Kristi learns why Babe stopped when she looked at the creek from Babe's point of view. This is the overall theme of the story—seeing something from a different point of view.**
   ○ Incorrect. The story does not say that you will become more relaxed if you learn to think like an animal.
   ○ Incorrect. The story does not say that parents will understand their children better if the family has animals.
   ○ Incorrect. The story does not say that you should become close friends with an animal.

2. ○ Incorrect. While Kristi knows some riders use whips and spurs, she also knows her father does not like to use these items while training a horse. Also, there is no indication that Kristi is trying to be different from her friends.
   ○ Incorrect. The story does not mention a fear of making the horse angry. Rather, Kristi knows her father chooses not to use whips and spurs.
   ○ Incorrect. The story does not mention Kristi's knowledge that Babe is smart and can figure out problems on her own.
   ● **Correct. Kristi's father trains horses, and he does not like to use whips and spurs. Kristi thinks her father is an excellent trainer, so she trusts his ideas.**

3. ● **Correct. To *snort* is to make a sound from the nose. *Sniffed* and *snorted* have very similar meanings.**
   ○ Incorrect. *Sneezed* and *snorted* do not mean the same thing. Both have to do with the nose, but in different ways.

○ Incorrect. *Bucked* and *snorted* do not mean the same thing. To *buck* would be to rear up or to try to throw the rider.
○ Incorrect. *Trotted* and *snorted* do not mean the same thing at all.

4. ○ Incorrect. There is no way to know that the next time Kristi has trouble with her horse she will need to walk her horse through a stream. It could be an entirely different problem.
   ● **Correct. Kristi's father wanted her to learn to think like a horse. That is how she solved her problem with Babe. She is likely to try the same method because she was successful the first time.**
   ○ Incorrect. Kristi may not be riding with her father the next time she has trouble on a horse.
   ○ Incorrect. Kristi does not use a whip or spurs to urge her horse on because her father does not approve of them.

5. ● **Correct. *Determined* means "strong-minded." It means about the same as *firm*.**
   ○ Incorrect. *Different* means "not alike." It does not mean the same as *firm*.
   ○ Incorrect. *Open* in this sense means "willing to change." It does not mean the same as *firm*.
   ○ Incorrect. *Weak* means "not strong." It does not mean the same as *firm*.

6. ○ Incorrect. Kristi's father is not hard to talk to. Kristi looks up to her father and listens to his advice.
   ● **Correct. Kristi's father is smart to let her figure out how to solve her own problem and he is kind to the horses.**
   ○ Incorrect. Kristi's father does understand her problem, but he wants her to solve it herself.
   ○ Incorrect. Kristi's father seems to love riding, but the passage does not portray him as always laughing.

Desert Wildlife (pages 9–11)

7. ○ Incorrect. The introduction lets you know what the passage will be about. It does not help you find information about how animals survive the desert heat.

○ Incorrect. The title is simple, and it only gives you an idea about the subject of the article. It does not tell you how animals survive the desert heat.

● **Correct. The headings tell you what type of information will follow. A heading called "Staying Cool" tells you how animals survive the desert heat.**

○ Incorrect. The drawing shows some of the animals that live in desert, but it does not tell you how animals survive the desert heat.

8. ○ Incorrect. There is no information in the article that says American deserts are growing larger.

○ Incorrect. The article says "some birds build their homes in cactus." The article does not say that all birds build their homes in cactus.

● **Correct. The article says many times that desert animals have adjusted very well to their environment. Desert animals can stay cool during the heat. It makes sense that they can stay warm during the cold nights.**

○ Incorrect. The article talks about different types of small animals, but it does not say that they are the most abundant animals in the desert.

9. ○ Incorrect. *Run* means "go faster than walking." It does not make sense to put *run* in place of the word *adapted*.

○ Incorrect. *Seen* is a past form of the verb "see." It does not make sense to put *seen* in place of the word *adapted*.

● **Correct. *Adjusted* means "got used to." It means about the same as *adapted*.**

○ Incorrect. *Surrendered* means "gave up." It does not make sense to put *surrendered* in place of the word *adapted*.

10. ○ Incorrect. There is no mention of the coyote being able to store water in its body.

○ Incorrect. There is no mention of the kangaroo rat being able to store water in its body.

○ Incorrect. There is no mention of the mule deer being able to store water in its body.

● **Correct. The article states, "The desert tortoise can store about a quart of water in its bladder, so it has a supply whenever it needs to drink."**

11. ○ Incorrect. *Pippi Longstocking* is the title of a book, so it should be italicized and not underlined. If the name of the book had been written by hand, it would be okay to underline it.

● **Correct. *Pippi Longstocking* is the title of a book, so it should be italicized.**

○ Incorrect. *Pippi Longstocking* is the title of a book, so it should be italicized, not put in quotation marks. The names of chapters can be put in quotation marks.

○ Incorrect. *Pippi Longstocking* is the title of a book, so it should be just be italicized. It should not also be put in quotation marks.

12. ○ Incorrect. The words *members* and *wildlife rescue* should be capitalized. *Members* is the first word of a quotation. *Wildlife Rescue* is the name of an organization.

○ Incorrect. The words *wildlife rescue* should be capitalized. *Wildlife Rescue* is the name of an organization.

○ Incorrect. The word *members* should be capitalized. The first word of a quotation should be capitalized.

● **Correct. The words *members* and *wildlife* rescue should be capitalized. *Members* is the first word of a quotation. *Wildlife Rescue* is the name of an organization.**

13. ○ Incorrect. This choice is not divided correctly. While the word does have three syllables, or parts with vowel sounds, the *h* should be included in the second syllable.
    ○ Incorrect. This choice is not divided correctly. The word has three syllables, not two.
    ● **Correct. This choice is divided correctly. Syllables are word parts that each contain vowel sounds.**
    ○ Incorrect. This choice is not divided correctly. The word has three syllables, not two.

14. ● **Correct. This sentence shows possession of both Trent's mother and the dog's food.**
    ○ Incorrect. This sentence does not show possession of Trent's mother or of the dog's food.
    ○ Incorrect. This sentence does not show possession of the dog's food.
    ○ Incorrect. This sentence incorrectly places the apostrophe after the *s* in the words *Trent's mother*.

Test 2

To March (pages 14–16)

1. ○ Incorrect. Because of the way the speaker greets March, you know that the speaker welcomes March.
   ○ Incorrect. The speaker wants April to leave, not March.
   ● **Correct. The speaker asks March to come in and is happy to see March.**
   ○ Incorrect. The way the speaker talks to March lets the reader know that they have met before.

2. ○ Incorrect. The poem does not refer to seasons.
   ● **Correct. The author loves to welcome March and dislikes the arrival of April.**

   ○ Incorrect. Only two months are mentioned in the poem, and the author doesn't like April.
   ○ Incorrect. The author welcomes March into her house, but she does not mention seasons.

3. ○ Incorrect. The line only shows how "glad" the speaker, a real person, is.
   ● **Correct. Maples are trees, not people. In the poem, maples seem to act like people who "know."**
   ○ Incorrect. This line does not treat the color purple as a person.
   ○ Incorrect. The speaker just refers to him- or herself again.

4. ○ Incorrect. The speaker does not forget anyone or anything.
   ○ Incorrect. It does not make sense that the reader would "demand" or want something in this sentence.
   ● **Correct. The word "state" means "to make known." It is the closest match for the definition of "declare."**
   ○ Incorrect. Although the speaker does like March, the use of the word "admire" does not make sense in this sentence.

5. ○ Incorrect. Because of the friendly way the speaker treats March, the speaker would not send March away.
   ○ Incorrect. The speaker tells March to lock the door when April knocks.
   ○ Incorrect. There is no indication that the speaker wants March to leave with April. The speaker is telling March to lock the door.
   ● **Correct. The speaker tells March to lock the door and to keep April out.**

The Bugs that Aren't (pages 17–20)

6. ○ Incorrect. This is not an effect of a pill bug putting its tail "fin" in water. Rather, it is a cause.

   ● **Correct. This is an effect of a pill bug putting its tail "fin" in water. The water moves up the pill bug's legs and up to its mouth, so it can drink.**

   ○ Incorrect. While pill bugs do seem to enjoy one another's odors, this is not an effect of a pill bug putting its tail "fin" in water.

   ○ Incorrect. This is not an effect of a pill bug putting its tail "fin" in water. Rather, this is an effect of the ground being too wet.

7. ○ Incorrect. Studying the title would not help you find information about what people used to think about pill bugs.

   ○ Incorrect. The first section heading is called "The Wet Life." Nothing in the section heading indicates that the section may tell about what people used to think of pill bugs.

   ○ Incorrect. The second section heading is called "Little Sips." Nothing in the section heading indicates that the section may tell about what people used to think of pill bugs.

   ● **Correct. This section is called "Old Beliefs," and it makes sense that this section may tell what people used to think about pill bugs.**

8. ○ Incorrect. The title of the article is "The Bugs That Aren't." Therefore, the title does not let the reader know anything about pill bugs and water.

   ● **Correct. Because the title of the article is "The Bugs That Aren't," the reader knows that pill bugs are not really bugs at all. The article tells us that they are crustaceans.**

   ○ Incorrect. The title does not say that all bugs are crustaceans.

   ○ Incorrect. The title does not say there are no pill bugs. It suggests that pill bugs are not named correctly.

9. ● **Correct. Bunching up together is one way pill bugs save water.**

   ○ Incorrect. While pill bugs do follow one another's scents, this is not something that causes pill bugs to save water.

   ○ Incorrect. The article specifically says that pill bugs do not live in water.

   ○ Incorrect. The article says that pill bugs do roll themselves into a ball, but not to save water.

10. ● **Correct. The word *parts* is closely related to the word *segments*. It fits in the sentence as a substitute for the word *segments*.**

    ○ Incorrect. The word *bodies* is not related to the word *segments*. It does not work in the sentence as a substitute for the word *segments*. The word *bodies* suggests a whole, and *segments* suggests parts.

    ○ Incorrect. The word *insects* is not related to the word *segments*. *Segments* are not insects.

    ○ Incorrect. The word *arms* is not related to the word *segments*. *Segments* are not arms.

11. ○ Incorrect. A *bibliography* is not a place where books are kept. That is a library. The definition does not fit in the example sentence. From the sentence, you can tell that the bibliography is in the book Madison read.

    ○ Incorrect. A *bibliography* is not a hobby of collecting rare books. The definition does not fit in the example sentence.

    ○ Incorrect. A *bibliography* is not a book about a person's life. That is a biography. The definition does not fit in the example sentence.

    ● **Correct. A *bibliography* is a list of books related to a single subject, and usually found at the end of a book. The definition fits in the example sentence.**

Answers and Explanations for Instruction

12. ○ Incorrect. This sentence leaves out the information about the park, and it makes it sound as if the dog is walking himself.

○ Incorrect. This sentence leaves out the information that Sally walks the dog. Instead, it sounds as if the dog walks by itself.

○ Incorrect. None of the original information suggests that Sally walks her dog every week. This is added information.

● **Correct. This sentence combines all of the information in one clear sentence.**

13. ○ Incorrect. The sentence is not clear. It doesn't make sense.

● **Correct. This sentence is clear. You know that the hikers climbing the hill are happy to see their cars.**

○ Incorrect. The sentence is not written clearly. It is awkward.

○ Incorrect. The sentence is not written clearly. It is written in such a way that it sounds as if the cars are climbing the hill instead of the hikers.

14. ○ Incorrect. The phrase *before the boat* doesn't make sense in this sentence.

● **Correct. The sentence says that the sailor is already on board the boat. This is the option that makes the most sense.**

○ Incorrect. This phrase makes it sound as if the sailor is running inside the boat, but you know from the sentence that he is on deck.

○ Incorrect. The sailor is on deck, so he cannot be under the boat.

15. ○ Incorrect. The word *noisy* should be written *noisily*.

○ Incorrect. The word *total* should be written *totally*.

○ Incorrect. The word *quiet* should be written *quietly*.

● **Correct. This sentence is written correctly. The adverb *carefully* tells how the girl put the bird in the nest.**

Test 3

(pages 23–29)

Sample Answer:
Title: Celebrating a Birthday

My very favorite birthday party was last year when I turned 9. I was in the fourth grade. My mom and dad asked me what I wanted to do for my birthday. I said that I wanted to have a movie party with pizza and ice cream. I love going to the movies, so I couldn't think of anything better to do with my friends than go to see a great movie and then eat pizza afterwards.

My birthday was on a Saturday in October, and I woke up really excited that day. We invited everyone to meet us at the movie theater for the 4:00 show. There was a great adventure film called *Oceans in the Sky* that had just opened the day before. My parents called the movie theater ahead of time, and the staff reserved the first two rows of the balcony for my party. Then they gave everyone a small popcorn and drink. The movie was great, and I loved seeing it with all my friends.

After the movie, we all went back to my house and ate pizza. We had every kind you could think of. My parents really went all out. My friends love pizza as much as I do, so they had a good time. I even decided to be daring and try a piece of pizza with pineapple on it. It wasn't that bad. After the pizza we all made our own ice cream sundaes. We had three different flavors of ice cream and then tons of toppings—nuts, cherries, whipped cream, crumbled cookies, and sprinkles. I felt really happy and excited all day. My friends seemed to have a good time, too. I think the best thing about this birthday celebration was being able to choose exactly what I wanted to do for my birthday. It was great to invite all my friends along, too.

Answers will vary. Use the rubrics on pages 32–34 to score students' responses.

Test 4

Happily Ever After (pages 30–33)

1. ● **Correct. *Unsteadily* means about the same as *shakily*. You can substitute *shakily* in the place of *unsteadily* in the sentence, and it makes sense.**
   ○ Incorrect. *Unsteadily* does not mean *angrily*. The word *angrily* does not fit in the sentence. You can tell by putting it in the place of *unsteadily*. It does not make sense in this sentence.
   ○ Incorrect. *Unsteadily* does not mean *carefully*. The word *carefully* does not fit in the sentence. You can tell by putting it in the place of *unsteadily*. It does not make sense in this sentence.
   ○ Incorrect. *Unsteadily* does not mean *gracefully*. The word *gracefully* does not fit in the sentence. You can tell by putting it in the place of *unsteadily*. It does not make sense in this sentence because you know that Rowena is not being graceful.

2. ○ Incorrect. Rowena does not do things like other people. Therefore, the theme "there is only one right way to do things" is not correct.
   ○ Incorrect. While Rowena is learning how to skate, this is not the main event of the story, so "learning new things helps people grow" is not the theme.
   ○ Incorrect. "Maintaining order and control" is clearly not the theme. We know this because Rowena is the main character, and her life is not one of order and control.
   ● **Correct. "Unplanned events can be exciting and enjoyable" is the main lesson, or theme, of the story. Rowena's unique approach to life is never dull, and many of the people around her find it exciting and enjoyable.**

3. ○ Incorrect. This sentence does not contain a comparison of two things using *like* or as.
   ○ Incorrect. This sentence does not contain a comparison of two things using *like* or *as*.
   ○ Incorrect. This sentence does not contain a comparison of two things using *like* or *as*.
   ● **Correct. This sentence compares the purple and green balloons to giant grapes and uses the word *like*.**

4. **Possible answer:**
   1) Rowena cooks the rice that is to be thrown at the wedding.
   2) Rowena made a birthday cake for Bert that was chocolate-mint-rainbow-iced cake, topped with purple pandas and sparklers.

   Answers will vary. Use the rubric on page 37 to score students' responses.

5. **Possible answer:**
   Rowena is unique. She made a chocolate-mint-rainbow-iced cake, topped with purple pandas and sparklers for Bert's birthday.
   Rowena is helpful and considerate. She makes the rice without being asked. She makes sure Mrs. Bidgely doesn't need any help before she leaves the bakery. She buys Bert a snow cone to thank him for teaching her how to skate.

   Answers will vary. Use the rubric on page 37 to score students' responses.

Answers and Explanations for Instruction

Zoo in the Sky (pages 34–40)

6. ○ Incorrect. The article is not an opinion paper. It is an informational piece.

   ○ Incorrect. The article is not written in list form, nor is it a cause/effect paper.

   ● **Correct. The article is a scientific description of nebulae and stars. Detail is given about how stars are born and how nebulae move.**

   ○ Incorrect. The article does not compare the facts about nebulae and stars to each other throughout the piece.

7. ○ Incorrect. This sentence does not give human qualities to a nonhuman thing.

   ○ Incorrect. This sentence does not give human qualities to a nonhuman thing.

   ○ Incorrect. This sentence does not give human qualities to a nonhuman thing.

   ● **Correct. This sentence gives human qualities to stars. It suggests that the stars can "behave" the same way that people behave.**

8. ○ Incorrect. The title is *Zoo in the Sky*. This does not tell you how stars are formed.

   ● **Correct. The heading "Star Birth" is the most likely place in the article to find information about how stars are born.**

   ○ Incorrect. Looking for the first place the word *star* is used in the article will probably not give you the information you need.

   ○ Incorrect. Reading the information under the heading "Huge Clouds" will most likely talk about really big clouds and not how stars are born.

9. ● **Correct. This is an opinion because it expresses the author's feeling, and it cannot be proven to be true.**

   ○ Incorrect. This is not an opinion; it is a fact. It can be proven.

   ○ Incorrect. This is not an opinion; it is a fact. It can be proven.

   ○ Incorrect. This is not an opinion; it is a fact. It can be proven.

10. **Possible answer:**

    I think the author chose the title *Zoo in the Sky* because he says that there are nebulae in the sky that look like different kinds of animals. A zoo is a place where you can see many different animals, and the sky is a place where you can see different animal shapes. He says that you can look into the sky and see the shapes of a pelican, a crab, a swan, and a horsehead.

    Answers will vary. Use the rubric on page 37 to score students' responses.

11. **Possible answer:**

    By using a telescope and studying the night sky, people can see star formations that look like different animals. These are called constellations. There are also patches of light in the night sky known as nebulae. These are clouds of gas and dust. Some nebulae are where stars are born, and others are where stars die. All nebulae are made of star material. Hydrogen gas, helium gas, and dust make up the nebulae where stars are born. Nebulae where stars die have outer layers of thin gaseous shells. These nebulae also contain white dwarfs. This is the name for the stars' shrunken centers, which are very hot. Sometimes when stars die, they explode. This violent event is known as a supernova.

    Answers will vary. Use the rubrics on pages 34–36 to score students' responses.

PRACTICE TEST

Each item on the Practice Test is correlated to an Indiana English/Language Arts Standard, which appears in boldface type before the answer and explanation.

Test 1

The Secret Garden (pages 45–48)

1. **4.2.3 Make and confirm predictions about text by using prior knowledge and ideas presented in the text itself, including illustrations, titles, topic sentences, important words, foreshadowing clues (clues that indicate what might happen next), and direct quotations.**

   - ● **Correct. This is the most likely prediction. The story talks about the key and Mary's plans for what to do in the garden whenever she is able to enter it.**
   - ○ Incorrect. The story does not talk about Mary returning to India.
   - ○ Incorrect. The story does not talk about Mary becoming a gardener. All Mary wants to do is enter and explore the garden.
   - ○ Incorrect. The story does not talk about Mary capturing the robin.

2. **4.3.2 Identify the main events of the plot, including their causes and the effects of each event on future actions, and the major theme from the story action.**

   - ○ Incorrect. While Mary does see a robin, this is not the most important event in the story.
   - ● **Correct. Mary finds a key. The story describes how she feels and what she thinks about the key and the secret garden. The key is talked about throughout the passage.**
   - ○ Incorrect. The story does not mention Mary making a new friend.
   - ○ Incorrect. Mary does not play in the garden, but she thinks about playing in the garden in the future, if she's ever able to find the gate.

3. **4.3.3 Use knowledge of the situation, setting, and a character's traits, motivations, and feelings to determine the causes for that character's actions.**

   - ● **Correct. As the story states, "she was not a child who had been trained to ask permission or consult her elders about things. All she thought about the key was that if it was the key to the closed garden, and she could find out where the door was, she could perhaps open it and see what was inside the walls. . . ." Mary is very interested in finding out what is inside the walls. She will certainly go in if she can find the door.**
   - ○ Incorrect. The story does not talk about any of Mary's friends.
   - ○ Incorrect. The story does not say that Mary plans to bury the key.
   - ○ Incorrect. The story states, "she was not a child who had been trained to ask permission or consult her elders about things." That means she did not usually ask for permission before doing something.

4. **4.1.6 Distinguish and interpret words with multiple meanings (*quarters*) by using context clues (the meaning of the text around a word).**

   - ● **Correct. *Walk* has many different meanings, but in this sentence, the girl is walking on a pathway or sidewalk.**
   - ○ Incorrect. "Taking the dog for a walk" is one way of using the word *walk*, but it is not the way it was used in this sentence.
   - ○ Incorrect. "Movement on foot" is the most common way of using the word *walk*, but it is not the way it is used in the sentence.
   - ○ Incorrect. "Behaving in a certain way" is a more unusual use of the word *walk*, and it is not the correct use in this sentence.

5. **4.1.2 Apply knowledge of synonyms (words with the same meaning), antonyms (words with opposite meanings), homographs (words that are spelled the same but have different meanings), and idioms (expressions that cannot be understood just by knowing the meanings of the words in the expression, such as _couch potato_) to determine the meaning of words and phrases.**

   ○ Incorrect. "Fighting with the wind had stirred her blood" does not mean "taking long hikes kept her warm." This definition does not fit within the context of the sentence.

   ○ Incorrect. "Fighting with the wind had stirred her blood" does not mean "exercising had helped to calm her down." This definition does not fit within the context of the sentence.

   ○ Incorrect. "Fighting with the wind had stirred her blood" does not mean "feeling angry had caused her to misbehave." This definition does not fit within the context of the sentence.

   ● **Correct. "Fighting with the wind had stirred her blood" means "being in new surroundings had made her feel more active." This definition fits within the context of the sentence.**

Earthquakes (pages 49–52)

6. **4.2.6 Distinguish between cause and effect and between fact and opinion in informational text.**

   ○ Incorrect. Landslides and mudslides are effects of earthquakes, not causes.

   ● **Correct. Stresses in underlying rocks cause earthquakes.**

   ○ Incorrect. Friction holding rocks in place does not cause earthquakes. It prevents them. However, when the rocks finally snap and move past each other, this is the focus of an earthquake.

   ○ Incorrect. Buildings fall down during earthquakes, but this is an effect of an earthquake, not a cause.

7. **4.2.2 Use appropriate strategies when reading for different purposes.**

   ○ Incorrect. Texas has very few earthquakes; the southern part of the state has never recorded an earthquake.

   ○ Incorrect. Florida has very few earthquakes; the southern part of the state has never recorded an earthquake.

   ○ Incorrect. Alabama has very few earthquakes; the southern part of the state has never recorded an earthquake.

   ● **Correct. Most earthquakes in the United States occur in California.**

8. **4.1.2 Apply knowledge of synonyms (words with the same meaning), antonyms (words with opposite meanings), homographs (words that are spelled the same but have different meanings), and idioms (expressions that cannot be understood just by knowing the meanings of the words in the expression, such as _couch potato_) to determine the meaning of words and phrases.**

   ○ Incorrect. _Burning_ means "on fire." It does not mean the same as _colliding_.

   ● **Correct. _Bumping_ means "to hit" or "knock into." It means about the same as _colliding_.**

   ○ Incorrect. _Standing_ means "getting up." It does not mean the same as _colliding_.

   ○ Incorrect. _Smoothing_ means "making flat or level." It does not mean the same as _colliding_.

9. **4.3.5 Define figurative language, such as similes, metaphors, hyperbole, or personification, and identify its use in literary works.**

   ○ Incorrect. This sentence does not contain a comparison using the words _like_ or _as_.

   ● **Correct. A simile is a comparison between two things using the words _like_ or _as_. This sentence says the rocks are "like a stretched rubber band."**

   ○ Incorrect. This sentence does not contain a comparison using the words _like_ or _as_.

○ Incorrect. This sentence does not contain a comparison using the words *like* or *as*.

10. **4.1.6 Distinguish and interpret words with multiple meanings *(quarters)* by using context clues (the meaning of the text around a word).**

   ○ Incorrect. This is one definition for the word *shocks*, but it does not make sense in the context of this sentence.

   ● **Correct. The violent shaking is exactly what is being referred to in the discussion about the effects of earthquakes.**

   ○ Incorrect. People may go into "shock" after a serious accident, but this definition does not make sense in this sentence.

   ○ Incorrect. A "sudden surprise" can be considered a "shock," but this definition does not make sense in this sentence.

11. **4.2.7 Follow multiple-step instructions in a basic technical manual.**

   ○ Incorrect. This sentence does not fit here in the multiple-step instructions. The user should review the manual first.

   ○ Incorrect. This sentence does not fit here in the multiple-step instructions. The user should watch the tape as a final step.

   ● **Correct. This sentence fits here in the multiple-step instructions. The user needs to have a tape in the camera in order to record images.**

   ○ Incorrect. This sentence does not fit here in the multiple-step instructions. The user would not be able to focus the camera until the lens cover was off.

12. **4.6.5 Use parentheses to explain something that is not considered of primary importance to the sentence, commas in direct quotations *(He said, "I'd be happy to go.")*, apostrophes to show possession *(Jim's shoes, the dog's food)*, and apostrophes in contractions *(can't, didn't, won't)*.**

   ○ Incorrect. The apostrophe in the contraction *didn't* is in the wrong place.

   ○ Incorrect. There should be an apostrophe in the contraction *didn't*.

   ● **Correct. The apostrophe in *didn't* is in the right place.**

   ○ Incorrect. There should be an apostrophe in the contraction *didn't*, and no apostrophe in *clothes*.

13. **4.6.6 Use underlining, quotation marks, or italics to identify titles of documents.**

   ● **Correct. Titles of poems, when written by hand or by computer, should be indicated by quotation marks.**

   ○ Incorrect. The title of the poem should have quotation marks around it.

   ○ Incorrect. The title of the poem should have quotation marks around it. If it were the tile of a book, it would be italicized.

   ○ Incorrect. The title of the poem should be indicated by quotation marks, not quotation marks and italics.

14. **4.4.10 Review, evaluate, and revise writing for meaning and clarity.**

   ● **Correct. This sentence is the most clear. The girl dropped the eggs and butter on the floor because she was walking too quickly.**

   ○ Incorrect. This sentence is completely awkward and does not make sense as it is written.

   ○ Incorrect. This sentence incorrectly places the phrase *on the floor before* the girl trying to walk quickly. The eggs and butter are what landed on the floor.

○ Incorrect. This sentence does not make sense. If the girl had been that quick, she would have been able to catch the eggs and butter before they hit the floor.

15. **4.4.12 Revise writing by combining and moving sentences and paragraphs to improve the focus and progression of ideas.**

○ Incorrect. This is not the best way to combine the sentences. The sentence suggests that the dentist did not find any cavities because Prudy's tooth was hurting.

● **Correct. This is the best way to combine the sentences. The events are in the correct order, and the meaning of the sentence is clear.**

○ Incorrect. This is not the best way to combine the sentences. This sentence has the events in the wrong order. The sentence suggests that the dentist's tooth was hurting.

○ Incorrect. This sentence has the two most important events in the wrong order. Prudy's tooth hurt first, and then she went to the dentist.

Test 2

The Visitor (pages 56–58)

1. **4.2.3 Make and confirm predictions about text by using prior knowledge and ideas presented in the text itself, including illustrations, titles, topic sentences, important words, foreshadowing clues (clues that indicate what might happen next), and direct quotations.**

○ Incorrect. Nothing in the poem suggests that the speaker is a dog.

● **Correct. The speaker is probably a boy. He talks about his necktie, which is the best clue that the speaker is a boy.**

○ Incorrect. The speaker is probably not a mother. Mothers don't usually wear neckties. Additionally, the voice in the poem is that of a child.

○ Incorrect. Nothing in the poem suggests that the speaker is a monster. At the end of the poem, you still don't know who the visitor was.

2. **4.3.2 Identify the main events of the plot, including their causes and the effects of each event on future actions, and the major theme from the story action.**

○ Incorrect. This is an effect of the trouble, not a cause.

○ Incorrect. This is an effect of the trouble, not a cause.

○ Incorrect. This is an effect of the trouble, not a cause.

● **Correct. This is the cause of the trouble. The visitor, whoever it is, is the one making trouble for everyone.**

3. **4.2.3 Make and confirm predictions about text by using prior knowledge and ideas presented in the text itself, including illustrations, titles, topic sentences, important words, foreshadowing clues (clues that indicate what might happen next), and direct quotations.**

○ Incorrect. The poet draws a distinction between "rover" and the cat in the two lines. It cannot be the cat.

● **Correct. "Rover" is a common name for a dog. We know that it can't be a cat because the cat is mentioned in the second line. We also know it isn't an elephant or mouse.**

○ Incorrect. The first stanza mentions an elephant as reference to the size of the mysterious visitor. There are no elephants in the poem.

○ Incorrect. The first stanza mentions a mouse as reference to the size of the mysterious visitor. There are no mice in the poem.

4. **4.3.3 Use knowledge of the situation, setting, and a character's traits, motivations, and feelings to determine the causes for that character's actions.**

○ Incorrect. We don't know that the speaker wanted to take a bath. However, we do know that the visitor has done many things besides fill the tub with rocks.

● **Correct. This is the most likely reason the speaker became angry. The visitor had done many rude and mean things.**

○ Incorrect. There is no mention in the poem that the speaker had told the visitor not to come to the house.

○ Incorrect. While the speaker did have his shoes and socks stolen, he yelled at the visitor before this happened.

5. **4.1.2 Apply knowledge of synonyms (words with the same meaning), antonyms (words with opposite meanings), homographs (words that are spelled the same but have different meanings), and idioms (expressions that cannot be understood just by knowing the meanings of the words in the expression, such as *couch potato*) to determine the meaning of words and phrases.**

● **Correct. If you were to smooth the hat, you would touch it softly and handle it gently.**

○ Incorrect. The word *ruined* and the word *crushed* are closely related in meaning. If something is crushed, it may be ruined.

○ Incorrect. The word *destroyed* and the word *crushed* are related in meaning. If something has been *crushed*, it may have been destroyed.

○ Incorrect. The word *squeezed* and the word *crushed* are closely related in meaning. If something has been squeezed, it has been crushed.

Soaring with the Wind: The Bald Eagle (pages 59–62)

6. **4.2.6 Distinguish between cause and effect and between fact and opinion in informational text.**

○ Incorrect. This is a fact that can be proved.

● **Correct. This sentence is the opinion of the author. It is entirely possible that someone has mistaken an eagle for another type of bird.**

○ Incorrect. This is a fact that can be proved.

○ Incorrect. This is a fact that can be proved.

7. **4.1.4 Use common roots (*meter = measure*) and word parts (*therm = heat*) derived from Greek and Latin to analyze the meaning of complex words (*thermometer*).**

○ Incorrect. While eagles do have hollow bones, you do not learn this from the Latin word *rapere*.

○ Incorrect. While eagles do have strong feathers, you do not learn this from the Latin word *rapere*.

● **Correct. According to the article, *rapere* means "to grasp or seize by force."**

○ Incorrect. While eagles do eat mostly fish and water birds, you do not learn this from the Latin word *rapere*.

8. **4.2.6 Distinguish between cause and effect and between fact and opinion in informational text.**

○ Incorrect. Strong feathers are not an effect of overlapping feathers.

○ Incorrect. The feathers' shape is not an effect of their overlapping.

○ Incorrect. Feathers' weight is not an effect of their overlapping.

● **Correct. Because feathers overlap, there is a lot of air space between the feathers. This is what helps protect the bird from heat and cold.**

9. **4.1.2 Apply knowledge of synonyms (words with the same meaning), antonyms (words with opposite meanings), homographs (words that are spelled the same but have different meanings), and idioms (expressions that cannot be understood just by knowing the meanings of the words in the expression, such as *couch potato*) to determine the meaning of words and phrases.**

   ○ Incorrect. "Big and heavy" are unrelated to the meaning of the word *streamlined*.

   ○ Incorrect. This is one possible meaning of the word *streamlined*, but it does not make sense in the context of this sentence.

   ● **Correct. This is the best definition of the word *streamlined* in this sentence. The birds are "smoothly shaped" for flight. Their bodies are designed to fly.**

   ○ Incorrect. The word *streamlined* can sometimes mean to "modernize" something, but this definition does not make sense in the context of this sentence.

10. **4.2.1 Use the organization of informational text to strengthen comprehension.**

   ● **Correct. This is the best heading for the bubble given the information contained in it. All of the information relates to the "size" of bald eagles.**

   ○ Incorrect. This heading does not match the information in the bubble. None of the information is about the skeleton of the eagle.

   ○ Incorrect. This heading does not match the information in the bubble. None of the information is about the feathers on eagles.

   ○ Incorrect. This heading does not make sense given the information in the bubble. None of the information is about what kind of hunters the eagles are.

11. **4.4.10 Review, evaluate, and revise writing for meaning and clarity.**

   ○ Incorrect. The paragraph is not about how it is nice to have a dog around the house. This does not make sense as a concluding sentence.

   ○ Incorrect. This paragraph is not about making service dogs do tricks. This does not make sense as a concluding sentence.

   ○ Incorrect. This paragraph is not about where to get service dogs. This does not make sense as a concluding sentence.

   ● **Correct. This paragraph is about what service dogs offer, so this sentence makes sense. Also, the phrase "in addition" shows there is a transition to the end of the paragraph.**

12. **4.4.12 Revise writing by combining and moving sentences and paragraphs to improve the focus and progression of ideas.**

   ○ Incorrect. Sentence 3 and 4 are closely linked by the word *however*. Splitting them up makes the paragraph confusing.

   ● **Correct. Moving the sentence here improves the progression of ideas. This sentence is an explanation about why planes weren't used. That explanation should come before mention of the dog teams.**

   ○ Incorrect. The sentence would not make sense here because the dog teams have already been mentioned. The first thought would have been to use airplanes.

   ○ Incorrect. The sentence is unrelated to the dog teams and the resolution of the problem. The sentence would not make logical sense here.

13. **4.6.5 Use parentheses to explain something that is not considered of primary importance to the sentence, commas in direct quotations (*He said, "I'd be happy to go."*), apostrophes to show possession (*Jim's shoes, the dog's food*), and apostrophes in contractions (*can't, didn't, won't*).**

- ● **Correct. *Mr. Smith's* and *doesn't* are correctly punctuated here.**
- ○ Incorrect. The apostrophes are missing in *Mr. Smith's* and *doesn't*.
- ○ Incorrect. The apostrophe in the word *doesn't* is in the wrong place.
- ○ Incorrect. The apostrophe in *Mr. Smith's* is missing here.

14. **4.6.7 Capitalize names of magazines, newspapers, works of art, musical compositions, organizations, and the first word in quotations, when appropriate.**

- ○ Incorrect. The title of the magazine *Living Well* should be capitalized.
- ● **Correct. The title of the painting is capitalized correctly.**
- ○ Incorrect. Each word of the song should be capitalized.
- ○ Incorrect. The name of the group Mothers Against Hunger should be capitalized.

15. **4.6.8 Spell correctly roots (bases of words, such as *unnecessary*, *cowardly*), inflections (words like *care/careful/caring*), words with more than one acceptable spelling (like *advisor/adviser*), suffixes and prefixes (*-ly, -ness, mis-, un-*), and syllables (word parts each containing a vowel sound, such as *sur•prise* or *e•col•o•gy*).**

- ● **Correct. This is the correct way to spell *comfortable*.**
- ○ Incorrect. This is an incorrect spelling of the word.
- ○ Incorrect. This is an incorrect spelling of the word.
- ○ Incorrect. This is an incorrect spelling of the word.

Test 3

(pages 67–73)

4.4.2 Select a focus, an organizational structure, and a point of view based upon purpose, audience, length, and format requirements for a piece of writing.

4.5.5 Use varied word choices to make writing interesting.

4.5.6 Write for different purposes (information, persuasion) and to a specific audience or person.

4.6.3 Create interesting sentences by using words that describe, explain, or provide additional details and connections, such as adjectives, adverbs, appositives, participial phrases, prepositional phrases, and conjunctions.

Sample answer:
Title: **My Favorite Hobby**

Lots of people have hobbies. My dad likes to collect stamps. My mom loves to work in her garden. My sister enjoys playing the harmonica. My best friend is learning how to juggle. My favorite hobby is making scrapbooks.

Making scrapbooks is a great way to express yourself. A scrapbook can be about anything you choose. For example, you could make a scrapbook with pictures of your favorite movie stars, or you could fill one with your own artwork. You could make a scrapbook about your day-to-day life. This would be kind of like a journal, but it could include things you find, like pretty leaves or even interesting pieces of litter! You could also add letters or copies of e-mail, along with your own writing or pictures from magazines.

I like making scrapbooks because it's a great way to be creative. One of the best things about making a scrapbook is there are no rules to follow. You get to do whatever you want, however you want. It's fun to look back at scrapbooks I've made in the past. They help me remember things I did or ideas I had. It's also fun to see how I've changed, by looking at how my scrapbooks change.

Some people feel like they have too many hobbies already, so they don't want to try anything new. But it seems to me, no matter what you enjoy, you can make a scrapbook to showcase your interests. For example, if your favorite hobby is photography, you can make a scrapbook full of your photos, as well as your favorite photos by other people. You might also do some research and write notes in your scrapbook about ways to improve your photography. Or, if your favorite hobby is magic tricks, you could make a scrapbook that captures the history of magic shows. In the same book, you could write notes and draw pictures showing how you do your favorite tricks.

A hobby is something to do as a way to relax and enjoy yourself. For me, there's nothing more relaxing or fun than making a new scrapbook. One of my projects this year is to invite some of my favorite people to work on a scrapbook with me. I will fill the first few pages of the scrapbook, and then I will send it to one of the people who agreed to work on it with me. That person will add whatever she wants to add. Then I will give it to another friend. This way, I'll have a scrapbook that holds some of my favorite people's ideas and art. I can hardly wait to see it!

Answers will vary. Use the rubrics on pages 32–34 to score students' responses.

Test 4

from *Black Beauty* (pages 75–78)

1. **4.2.3 Make and confirm predictions about text by using prior knowledge and ideas presented in the text itself, including illustrations, titles, topic sentences, important words, foreshadowing clues (clues that indicate what might happen next), and direct quotations.**

   ● **Correct. Beauty is the young colt who talks about his early home with his mother.**

   ○ Incorrect. Duchess is Beauty's mother. She is not the one talking about her early home.

   ○ Incorrect. Dick is the plowboy throwing stones. It is not his early home.

   ○ Incorrect. Old Daniel is the man who looked after the horses. It is not his early home.

2. **4.3.3 Use knowledge of the situation, setting, and a character's traits, motivations, and feelings to determine the causes for that character's actions.**

   ○ Incorrect. Dick does eat blackberries, but there is no indication in the story that the master cares about this.

   ○ Incorrect. The master is not an impatient man. He is good and kind man.

   ○ Incorrect. While Dick is a plowboy, there is no mention in the story that he did not finish his work.

   ● **Correct. Dick was throwing stones at the horses to make them gallop. Sometimes the stones hit the horses. When the master saw this, he became very angry with Dick.**

3. **4.3.2 Identify the main events of the plot, including their causes and the effects of each event on future actions, and the major theme from the story action.**

○ Incorrect. There is no mention that Beauty doesn't like to work. His mother's advice includes telling him to always do his work with a good will.

○ Incorrect. Beauty's grandfather was a racehorse.

● **Correct. Beauty comes from a strong, kind family. His mother is sweet and his grandmother was also. His father has a good reputation, and his grandfather was a successful racehorse.**

○ Incorrect. There is no indication that Beauty's grandmother still lives on the farm.

4. **4.3.5 Define figurative language, such as similes, metaphors, hyperbole, or personification, and identify its use in literary works.**

○ Incorrect. Dick is a boy, so he cannot be an example of personification. He is already human.

○ Incorrect. Duchess is a horse, but the work she does during the day is work that horses, not people, do. Duchess working in the fields during the day is not an example of personification.

● **Correct. Personification is giving something that is nonhuman, such as a horse, human qualities. Beauty telling the story is an excellent example of personification.**

○ Incorrect. The Old Daniel is a man, so he cannot be an example of personification. He is already human.

5. **4.3.2 Identify the main events of the plot, including their causes and the effects of each event on future actions, and the major theme from the story action.**

Possible answers:
- The master gave the horses good lodging.
- The master gave the horses good food.
- The master spoke kindly to the horses.
- The master gave the horses snacks of bread and carrots.
- The master punished Dick and fired him after Dick threw stones at the horses.

Answers will vary. Use the rubric on page 37 to score students' responses.

6. **4.3.3 Use knowledge of the situation, setting, and a character's traits, motivations, and feelings to determine the causes for that character's actions.**

Possible answers:
- Beauty's father "has a great name in these parts."
- Beauty's grandfather "won the cup two years at the Newmarket races."
- Beauty's grandmother "has the sweetest temper of any horse" Beauty's mother ever knew.
- Beauty's mother Duchess says, "I think you have never seen me kick or bite."

Answers will vary. Use the rubric on page 37 to score students' responses.

Answers and Explanations for Instruction

Light Pollution (pages 79–86)

7. **4.2.6 Distinguish between cause and effect and between fact and opinion in informational text.**

   ○ Incorrect. This statement is a fact, which can be proven.

   ○ Incorrect. This statement is a fact, which can be proven.

   ● **Correct. This is an opinion, and not a fact that can be proven. Rather, it is a feeling or idea that the author has.**

   ○ Incorrect. This statement is a fact, which can be proven.

8. **4.1.4 Use common roots** *(meter = measure)* **and word parts** *(therm = heat)* **derived from Greek and Latin to analyze the meaning of complex words** *(thermometer).*

   ○ Incorrect. An astronomer is not a person who designs airplanes.

   ○ Incorrect. An astronomer is not a person who flies to outer space. That is an astronaut.

   ● **Correct. An astronomer is a scientist who studies stars and planets.**

   ○ Incorrect. An astronomer is not a scientist who studies plants and animals. That is a biologist.

9. **4.2.3 Make and confirm predictions about text by using prior knowledge and ideas presented in the text itself, including illustrations, titles, topic sentences, important words, foreshadowing clues (clues that indicate what might happen next), and direct quotations.**

   ○ Incorrect. Although oceans have little light pollution, the ocean's surface moves and would not be a good place to study stars.

   ● **Correct. A dark land area away from light pollution would be the best place to study stars.**

   ○ Incorrect. The bright Northern Lights would make it difficult to see and study the stars.

   ○ Incorrect. Light pollution from cities makes it difficult to see and study stars.

10. **4.2.1 Use the organization of informational text to strengthen comprehension.**

    ○ Incorrect. This section says that the same stars are in the sky now that were there when our ancestors could see them. But this is not the main idea of the section.

    ○ Incorrect. The section does say that there are billions of stars in the sky, but this is not the main idea of the section. The main idea is that those stars are hard to see because of light pollution.

    ● **Correct. This entire section is about how people have trouble seeing the stars because of light pollution. This section says that people who study the stars have trouble seeing them. People who are just looking up in the sky at night also have trouble seeing them.**

    ○ Incorrect. This section does not say that it would be easier to see where you are going at night if there weren't light pollution.

11. **4.2.2 Use appropriate strategies when reading for different purposes.**

    Possible answers:
    • Effect: star gazers can't see many stars; Solution: turn off outside lights; pass laws about light pollution
    • Effect: migrating birds are killed; Solution: turn off lights in tall buildings during nights of migration months

    Answers will vary. Use the rubric on page 37 to score students' responses.

12. **4.2.6 Distinguish between cause and effect and between fact and opinion in informational text.**

   Possible answers:
   - First Law: Outside lights must point down
   - How the first law helps decrease light pollution: the light does not shine up into the dark night sky
   - Second Law: People must use weaker lights
   - How the second law helps decrease light pollution: this keeps skies darker while saving energy

   Answers will vary. Use the rubric on page 37 to score students' responses.

13. **4.4.12 Revise writing by combining and moving sentences and paragraphs to improve the focus and progression of ideas.**

   4.5.4 Write summaries that contain the main ideas of the reading selection and the most significant details.

   4.6.1 Write smoothly and legibly in cursive, forming letters and words that can be read by others.

   Sample answer:
   Light pollution is when there is too much artificial light in the sky. This has negative effects, including preventing people from seeing the stars at night. Although it might sound silly, light pollu-tion can affect people's health. That is, too much man-made light can disturb the body's natural rhythm. This can change a person's mood and health. Also, not being able to see the stars makes an astronomer's work much more difficult.

Light pollution also affects animals. When birds are migrating, they frequently fly into tall buildings at night. This happens when the buildings have their lights on. The birds are drawn to the lights, but they can't see the glass, so they fly into it. Sea turtles also suffer from light pollution. They are born by the ocean. In the past, the brightest light was the light on the horizon, over the ocean. But now, man-made light confuses the newborn turtles, so instead of swimming into the water, they might wander off in the wrong direction and die.

Light pollution can be reduced. Some places have passed laws that restrict the use of lights at night. Rangers at national parks are also working to keep the skies over the wilderness dark. And bird-lovers are working to get the owners and tenants of tall buildings in big cities to turn off their lights at night when birds are migrating.

Answers will vary. Use the rubrics on pages 34–36 to score students' responses.

Scoring Rubric

Scoring your students' responses to the Test 3 writing activity and Test 4 short-response and extended-response items involves the use of four rubrics that rate students' mastery of specific reading, writing, and language skills standards.

Use the following rubrics to determine correct responses to short-response and extended-response items and the writing activity:

Modeled Instruction	
Writing Applications Rubric:	pages 26–29 (Test 3)
Language Conventions Rubric:	pages 26–29 (Test 3), pages 38–40 (item 11)
Extended-Response Writing Applications Rubric:	pages 39–40 (item 11)
Short-Response Rubric:	page 33 (item 4), page 33 (item 5), page 37 (item 10)
Practice Test	
Writing Applications Rubric:	pages 70–73 (Test 3)
Language Conventions Rubric:	pages 70–73 (Test 3), pages 84–86 (item 13)
Extended-Response Writing Applications Rubric:	pages 85–86 (item 13)
Short-Response Rubric:	page 78 (item 5), page 78 (item 6), page 83 (item 11), page 83 (item 12)

Writing Applications Overview

Overview of the Writing Applications Rubric

The Writing Applications Rubric summarizes the requirements for each of the six score levels. Read across the rows to determine a specific score point's criteria.

Score Level	Ideas and Content	Organization
6	• Accomplishes task fully • Thorough, relevant, and complete ideas are included	• Logically organizes ideas
5	• Accomplishes task fully • Many relevant ideas are included	• Logically organizes ideas
4	• Accomplishes task fully • Relevant ideas are included	• Logically organizes ideas
3	• Accomplishes task minimally	• Shows an attempt to logically organize ideas
2	• Accomplishes task partially	• Shows a minimal attempt to logically organize ideas
1	• Does not accomplish task • Very few relevant ideas are included	• Illogically organizes ideas

Score Level	Style	Voice
6	• Demonstrates exceptional word usage and writing technique	• Language used displays an exceptional knowledge of the audience
5	• Demonstrates very good word usage and writing technique	• Language used displays a very good knowledge of the audience
4	• Demonstrates good word usage and writing technique	• Language used displays a good knowledge of the audience
3	• Demonstrates ordinary word usage and average writing technique	• Language used displays an ordinary knowledge of the audience
2	• Demonstrates minimal word usage and writing technique	• Language used displays a minimal knowledge of the audience
1	• Demonstrates less than minimal word usage and writing technique	• Language used displays less than minimal knowledge of the audience

Writing Applications Rubric

SCORE POINT 6
Ideas and Content

The writing sample fully accomplishes the task by focusing on the topic and presenting a unified theme or main idea with no tangents. It includes thorough, relevant, and complete ideas by fully exploring facets of the topic and including in-depth information and developed supporting details.

Organization

The writing sample's ideas are logically organized and presented meaningfully as a cohesive whole. It has a beginning, middle, and end and progresses in a way that enhances meaning. Between ideas, sentences, and paragraphs, smooth transitions enhance the meaning of the text.

Style

The writing sample has exceptional word usage shown through the controlled use of challenging vocabulary words. The vocabulary is used to make precise, detailed explanations, rich descriptions, and clear, vivid actions. Exceptional writing techniques are shown through fluent writing. Varied sentence patterns, complex sentences too, are included. The writer's techniques like imagery/dialogue or humor/suspense are demonstrated.

Voice

The writing sample has language and tone effectively adjusted to task and reader. The voice exhibits the appropriate register and reflects a strong sense of audience. An original perspective is evident.

Language Conventions Rubric

Score 4	**A good command of language skills is shown in the writing sample.**
	A Score Point 4 paper will have infrequent errors that are of the first-draft kind; overall communication is only slightly affected. The flow of communication will not be impaired.
	Words have very few or no • capitalization errors • spelling errors **Sentences have few or no** • punctuation errors • grammar or word usage errors **Writing has very few or no** • paragraphing errors • run-on sentences

Score 3	**An adequate command of language skills is shown in the writing sample.**
	A Score Point 3 paper will have occasional errors, but these errors will not seriously impair the writer's meaning or flow of communication.
	Words have occasional • capitalization errors • spelling errors **Sentences have occasional** • punctuation errors • grammar or word usage errors **Writing has occasional** • paragraphing errors • run-on sentences

Score 2	**A minimal command of language skills is shown in the writing sample.**
	A Score Point 2 paper will have frequent errors that force the reader to stop and reread sections of the text. Communication will be impaired, but if the reader tries, he or she will be able to understand the writer's message.
	Words have frequent • capitalization errors • spelling errors **Sentences have frequent** • punctuation errors • grammar or word usage errors **Writing has frequent** • paragraphing errors • run-on sentences

Score 1	**A less than minimal command of language skills is shown in the writing sample.**
	A Score Point 1 paper will have numerous errors that are of a wide variety that prevent the reader from understanding the writer's message.
	Words have many • capitalization errors • spelling errors **Sentences have many** • punctuation errors • grammar or word usage errors **Writing has many** • paragraphing errors • run-on sentences

Extended-Response Writing Applications Overview

Score 4	What the writing sample does
	• accomplishes the task fully • includes many relevant ideas • logically organizes ideas • shows very good word usage • exhibits very good writing technique • effectively adjusts language and tone for reader and task
Score 3	What the writing sample does
	• accomplishes the task • includes relevant ideas • logically organizes ideas • shows good word usage • exhibits good writing technique • attempts to adjust language and tone for reader and task
Score 2	What the writing sample does
	• accomplishes the task minimally • includes some relevant ideas • attempts to logically organize ideas • shows ordinary word usage • exhibits adequate writing technique • attempts to adjust language and tone for reader and task
Score 1	What the writing sample does
	• accomplishes the task partially or not at all • includes few relevant ideas • minimally attempts to logically organize ideas • shows minimal word usage • exhibits minimal or less than minimal writing technique • has inappropriate language and tone for reader and task

Extended-Response Writing Applications Rubric

SCORE POINT 4
Ideas and Content

The writing sample fully accomplishes the task by focusing on the topic and presenting a unified theme or main idea with no tangents. It gives plenty of information and develops more than adequate supporting details in order to explore different facets of the topic.

Organization

The writing sample's ideas are logically organized and presented meaningfully as a cohesive whole. It has a beginning, middle, and end and progresses in a way that enhances meaning. Between ideas, sentences, and paragraphs, smooth transitions enhance the meaning of the text.

Style

The writing sample has very good word usage shown through the controlled use of vocabulary words. The vocabulary is used to make precise, detailed explanations, rich descriptions, and clear, vivid actions. Very good writing techniques are shown through fluent writing. Varied sentence patterns, complex sentences too, are included. The writer's techniques like imagery/dialogue or humor/suspense are demonstrated.

Voice

The writing sample has language and tone effectively adjusted to task and reader. The voice exhibits the appropriate register and reflects a strong sense of audience. An original perspective is evident.

Short-Response Rubric

The Short-Response Rubric is used to score the short-answer items that ask students for two pieces of information from a passage. If a student provides an answer that is not included in the list of sample exemplars, but the text supports the response, then the student should be given credit for the answer.

Short-Response Rubric	
Score 2	• Answer includes two exemplars from the passage
Score 1	• Answer includes one exemplar from the passage
Score 0	• Other

Teacher's Notes

A Butterfly Called Hope

by *NY Times* best-selling author
Mary Alice Monroe
with *Linda Love*
photography by Barbara J. Bergwerf

In my mother's garden there are many flowers: pink, blue, yellow and orange.

They open their petals to the sun.

I call them flying flowers.

monarch   cloudless sulphur   gulf fritillary   black swallowtail

I look at a green milkweed leaf
and see a bright yellow and black
bug staring back at me.

Chewing . . . chewing . . . chewing.

"Mommy, come quick! What is it? Will it bite me? Or sting me? Will it make me sick?"

"Don't be afraid," my mother says. "It won't hurt you. That is a caterpillar. Someday it will grow to be a beautiful butterfly."

"What kind of butterfly will it be?" I ask, still afraid.

My mother says, "Let's take the caterpillar to Nana Butterfly. She will know."

We place the caterpillar gently on a leaf in a big glass jar. I carry it in my lap in my mother's car.

Nana Butterfly looks in the jar. "You have a monarch caterpillar. You can leave it with me. I'll take good care of it and set the butterfly free."

"No," I tell her, because I love my caterpillar.

"I want to keep it. Mommy, can I please?"

Each morning I put clean paper towels on the bottom of the aquarium and add fresh milkweed from the garden.

Through the glass I can watch my caterpillar getting bigger and bigger.

All day it eats and grows and poops! Caterpillar poop is called *frass*.

I make sure my caterpillar has plenty of fresh milkweed to eat.

One day I do not see the caterpillar eating. I do not see it crawling. I do not see it at all.

"Mommy, come quick! Where is it?"

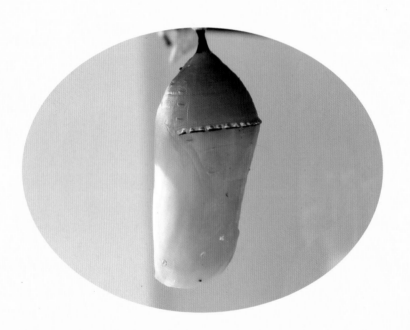

My mother points to a jade green chrysalis hanging at the top of the tank. She tells me, "The change is beginning!"

Eight days later, I see the chrysalis is now black.

"Mommy, come quick! What happened to my chrysalis? Is it sick?"

Mommy says, "Don't worry little one. Your butterfly is almost here. Come and look very closely. You can see the butterfly's wing!"

We watch . . . and wait . . .

. . . A new butterfly slowly emerges. She clings to her empty chrysalis. Her wings are soft and droop like a brilliant orange and black cape.

We watch her velvety wings slowly grow larger and larger. When she is ready, she tests them, fluttering one . . . two . . . three times.

My mother says, "It's time for her to fly!"

"No," I cry. "I want to keep my butterfly!"

"A butterfly needs to fly free to sip sweet nectar from flowers. She will lay eggs on milkweed leaves so there will be more butterflies."

"If you name your butterfly, wherever it goes, it will be yours."

"Can I give the butterfly *my* name?" I ask.

My mother smiles. "Yes, I think your name is perfect."

My monarch opens her wings to the sun, fluttering in joy. Then, on a soft breeze, my butterfly flies.

I feel the warm sun on my face as I call out,

"Your name is Hope!"

For Creative Minds

Monarch Life Cycle Sequencing

Put the descriptions of the butterfly life cycle stages in order to match the pictures.

The caterpillar eats and eats.

The chrysalis is complete and green.

The caterpillar hatches (larva stage).

The caterpillar starts to turn into a chrysalis.

The adult butterfly flies away and will lay eggs.

The butterfly starts to emerge from the chrysalis.

The adult lays eggs. Compare the egg size to the dime.

The chrysalis turns clear. We see black butterfly wings.

Answers: 1) Adult lays eggs. 2) The caterpillar hatches. 3) The caterpillar starts to turn into a chrysalis. 5) The green chrysalis is complete. 6) The chrysalis turns clear. 7) The butterfly emerges. 8) The butterfly flies away.

Butterfly Vocabulary Matching Activity

Match the word to the description.

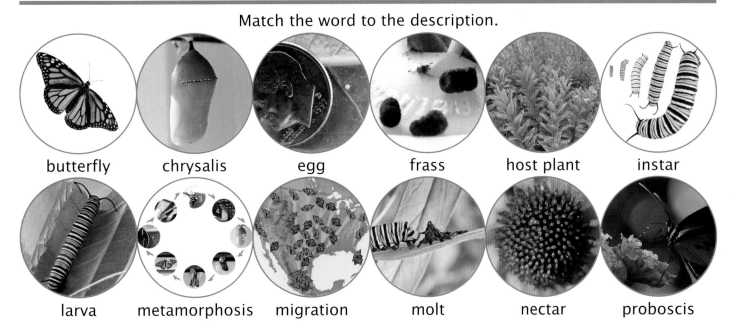

butterfly   chrysalis   egg   frass   host plant   instar

larva   metamorphosis   migration   molt   nectar   proboscis

1. This is the final and adult stage of this insect's life cycle.

2. This is the second stage of the life cycle when the caterpillar is an eating machine and grows. Under normal summer temperatures, this stage lasts from nine to fourteen days.

3. This is the "resting stage" during which a caterpillar changes into a butterfly. This third stage of development lasts ten to fourteen days under normal summer conditions and is also called "pupa."

4. This is laid by an adult female on a milkweed leaf and is the first stage of the life cycle.

5. A special word for caterpillar droppings (poop).

6. The only plants on which butterflies and other insects lay their eggs. Monarchs only use milkweed. There are over 100 types of milkweed. Other butterflies use other plants.

7. This is the time between molts of the caterpillar when the body grows. Monarch caterpillars have five.

8. This is a life-cycle change of an insect to an adult.

9. This journey from one location to another is usually to follow food sources and climate changes.

10. As a caterpillar grows, it sheds its outer layer of skin with a new, bigger skin underneath that will then harden.

11. The sugary juice made by flowers that is used as food by butterflies and other insects.

12. A butterfly uses this straw-like tongue to drink water and nectar. When not in use, the butterfly curls it up and keeps it out of the way.

Answers: 1) Butterfly, 2) Larva, 3) Chrysalis, 4) Egg, 5) Frass, 6) Host Plant, 7) Instar, 8) Metamorphosis, 9) Migration, 10) Molt, 11) Nectar, 12) Proboscis

Monarch Generations and Migrations

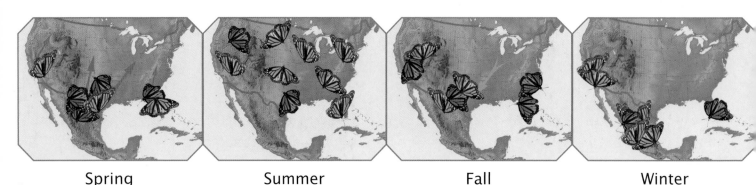

Spring   Summer   Fall   Winter

Most of us are familiar with birds migrating in the spring and fall. Did you know that some insects, like the monarch butterfly, migrate too?

The Generations

The generation that spent the winter in Mexico will fly north to look for milkweed. These monarchs will lay eggs and after a very long life, will die.

First generation—March and April: The eggs hatch into caterpillars, form chrysalises, and emerge as butterflies. These butterflies continue to migrate north to the area around where their parents hatched, laying eggs along the way.

Second generation—May, June and July: The eggs hatch into caterpillars, form chrysalises, and emerge as butterflies.

Third generation—July and August: The eggs hatch into caterpillars, form chrysalises, emerge as butterflies, and then lay their eggs.

Fourth generation—August, September and October: The eggs hatch into caterpillars, form chrysalises, and emerge as butterflies. Depending on the population to which they belong, monarchs migrate south to Southern California or Mexico where it is warm enough for them to survive the winter. Even though these butterflies have never been there before, they somehow find their way and usually even go to the same trees as their great-grandparents! Once there, the butterflies stay through the winter. Monarchs in Florida do not migrate. Some scientists are studying whether some "East Coast" monarchs migrate to Florida instead of Mexico.

Fourth generation (still)—February and March: Monarch butterflies start flying north again and lay their eggs. The cycle starts again!

Raising Monarchs

You will need a safe habitat for the caterpillars and lots of fresh milkweed. You should use milkweed that is native to your area. For more detailed information, please go to the "teaching activities" by clicking on the book's cover at SylvanDellPublishing.com.

Caring for the caterpillars:

Monarch caterpillars are very hungry but they *only* eat milkweed leaves! Add leaves to the habitat daily. When the caterpillars get bigger, they will eat a lot, so be sure to check often and add leaves as needed.

Keep the leaves moist by adding water to small containers or wrap the ends in a damp paper towel. If they are not fresh, keep extra milkweed leaves in a plastic bag in the refrigerator.

Keep the habitat clean by removing the frass and dried leaves and changing the paper towels often.

Things to watch for:

If your caterpillar wanders off and stops moving, do not disturb it. It is molting.

Don't let your caterpillars get too crowded or your habitat dirty. Bacteria can form that can make your caterpillars sick.

After 10-14 days, your large caterpillar will stop eating and wander to the top of the habitat. First it will spin a silk knot, then tuck its feet in, and hang head down. It looks like a "J." After about 14 hours, it will begin to twist and do a "pupa dance" as it changes into a pale green chrysalis.

About two weeks later, the chrysalis will look black. This means that your butterfly will emerge in about 24 hours!

Monarchs usually emerge early in the morning—it happens fast so don't miss it! The butterfly will pop out and hang on the chrysalis shell for two hours while it pumps fluid into the wings. You can watch the wings grow. This is a dangerous time for a butterfly. If it falls, or if it is touched, the wings will be damaged and it won't fly. The new butterfly will hang for several hours while the wings dry.

Three to four hours after the butterfly emerges it is safe to release to the garden. The butterfly doesn't eat until the day after it is born, so if it is raining, you can keep your butterfly in a flight cage for a day or two.

Release the butterfly in your garden where there are flowers. If you live in a city, you can release the butterfly in a park or a garden center, but be sure not to release it where people have sprayed pesticides.

Thanks to Karen Oberhauser, Director of Monarchs in the Classroom Program and President of the Monarch Butterfly Sanctuary Foundation; and to Trecia Neal, biologist at the Fernbank Science Center and Monarchs Across Georgia for verifying the accuracy of the information in this book.

Library of Congress Cataloging-in-Publication Data

Monroe, Mary Alice, author.
  A butterfly called Hope / by NY Times best-selling author Mary Alice Monroe, with Linda Love ; photography by Barbara J. Bergwerf.
      pages cm
  Audience: 4-9.
  Audience: K to grade 3.
  ISBN 978-1-60718-854-4 (hardcover English) -- ISBN 978-1-60718-856-8 (pbk. English) -- ISBN 978-1-60718-857-5 (downloadable (pdf) ebook) -- ISBN 978-1-60718-859-9 (interactive web-based ebook) -- ISBN 978-1-60718-858-2 (downloadable (pdf) Spanish ebook)
  1. Monarch butterfly--Juvenile literature. 2. Butterflies--Juvenile literature. 3. Caterpillars--Juvenile literature. 4. Metamorphosis--Juvenile literature. I. Love, Linda, 1944- author. II. Bergwerf, Barbara J., illustrator. III. Title.
  QL561.D3M664 2013
  595.78'9--dc23
                              2013013641

Translated into Spanish by Rosalyna Toth: Una mariposa llamada Esperanza

Lexile® Level: 430
Educator keywords: butterfly life cycle, metamorphosis

Manufactured in China, June 2013
This product conforms to CPSIA 2008
First Printing

Sylvan Dell Publishing
Mt. Pleasant, SC 29464
www.SylvanDellPublishing.com